D0845452

Israel

by Thomas Persano

Consultant: Marjorie Faulstich Orellana, PhD
Professor of Urban Schooling
University of California, Los Angeles

New York, New York

Credits

Cover, © asiseeit/iStock and © stellalevi/iStock; TOC, © Mickyso/Shutterstock; 4, © Leonid Andronov/Shutterstock; 5T, © Maurizio Bersanelli/Panther Media/AGE Fotostock; 5B, © Max Topchili/Shutterstock; 7, © anouchka/iStock; 8, © BibleLandPictures.com/Alamy; 9, © Noam Armonn/Alamy; 10T, © Ondrej Chvatal/Shutterstock; 10B, © haimtaragan/iStock; 11, © Artemy Voihansky/CC BY-SA 4.0; 12–13, © vvvita/iStock; 13T, © Oleg Golovnev/Shutterstock; 14, © MaestroBooks/iStock; 15, © Ryan Rodrick Beiler/Shutterstock; 16, © robertharding/Alamy; 17, © sedmak/iStock; 18–19, © Rostislav Glinsky/Dreamstime; 19T, © -Taurus-/Shutterstock; 20, © Mendy Hechtman/Flash90/Redux Pictures; 21T, © PhotoStock-Israel/Alamy; 21B, © Moseva/iStock; 22T, © Alexander Dvorak/Shutterstock; 22B, © ChameleonsEye/Shutterstock; 23, © Yadid Levy/Alamy; 24T, © KarinaUrmantseva/iStock; 24B, © Klaus-Werner Friedrich/imageBROKER/Alamy; 25, © RoniMeshulamAbramovitz/iStock; 26–27, © dpa picture alliance archive/Alamy; 27R, © Imgorthand/iStock; 28T, © Walter Bibikow/AGE Fotostock; 28B, © ChameleonsEye/Shutterstock; 29, © Roberto Salomone/Mondadori Collection/AGE Fotostock; 30T, © Anton_Ivanov/Shutterstock, © Andrey Lobachev/Shutterstock, and © Radomir Tarasov/Dreamstime; 30B, © frantisekhojdysz/Shutterstock; 31 (T to B), © DeltaOFF/Shutterstock, © Sarawut Kundej/Shutterstock, © Monkey Business Images/Shutterstock, © ChameleonsEye/Shutterstock, and © Claudiad/iStock; 32, © tristan tan/Shutterstock.

Publisher: Kenn Goin
Senior Editor: Joyce Tavolacci
Creative Director: Spencer Brinker
Design: Debrah Kaiser
Photo Researcher: Thomas Persano

Library of Congress Cataloging-in-Publication Data

Names: Persano, Thomas, author. | Orellana, Marjorie Faulstich, consultant.
Title: Israel / by Thomas Persano ; consultant: Marjorie Faulstich Orellana,
    PhD, Professor of Urban Schooling, University of California, Los Angeles.
Description: New York, New York : Bearport Publishing Company, Inc., [2018] |
    Series: Countries we come from. | Includes bibliographical references and
    index.
Identifiers: LCCN 2017039224 (print) | LCCN 2017039615 (ebook) |
    ISBN 9781684025336 (ebook) | ISBN 9781684024759 (library)
Subjects: LCSH: Israel—Juvenile literature.
Classification: LCC DS126.5 (ebook) | LCC DS126.5 .P47 2018 (print) | DDC
    956.94—dc23
LC record available at https://lccn.loc.gov/2017039224

For more information, write to Bearport Publishing Company, Inc., 45 West 21st Street, Suite 3B, New York, New York 10010. Printed in the United States of America.

10 9 8 7 6 5 4 3 2 1

Contents

BUSTLING

Historic

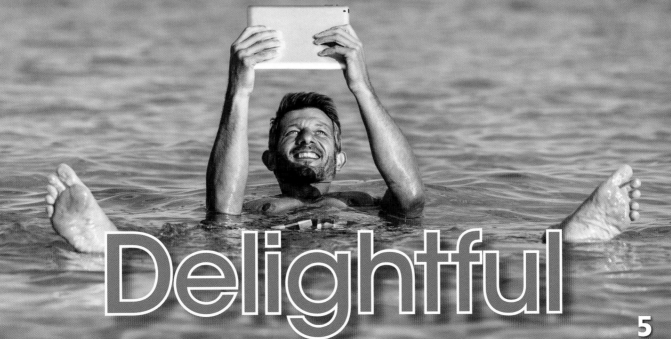

Delightful

Israel is a small country in the Middle East.

It's about the same size as New Jersey.

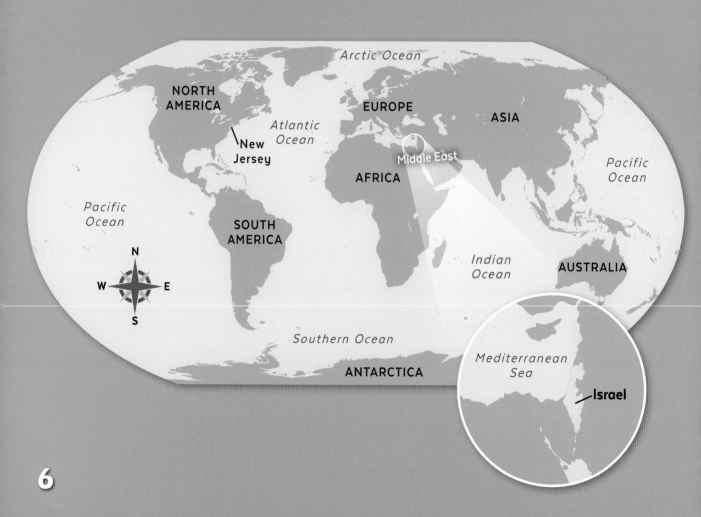

More than 8 million people live in Israel.

7

Snowy mountains rise in northern Israel.

Mt. Hermon

Israel's highest mountain is Mt. Hermon.

A huge desert covers the southern part of the country.

The Negev Desert stretches over half of Israel.

It's home to hyenas, ibexes, and other animals.

hyena

ibex

Many unusual birds live there, too.

hoopoe

The hoopoe is the **national** bird of Israel.

The Dead Sea is a huge salt lake in Israel.

People like to bathe in the cool waters.

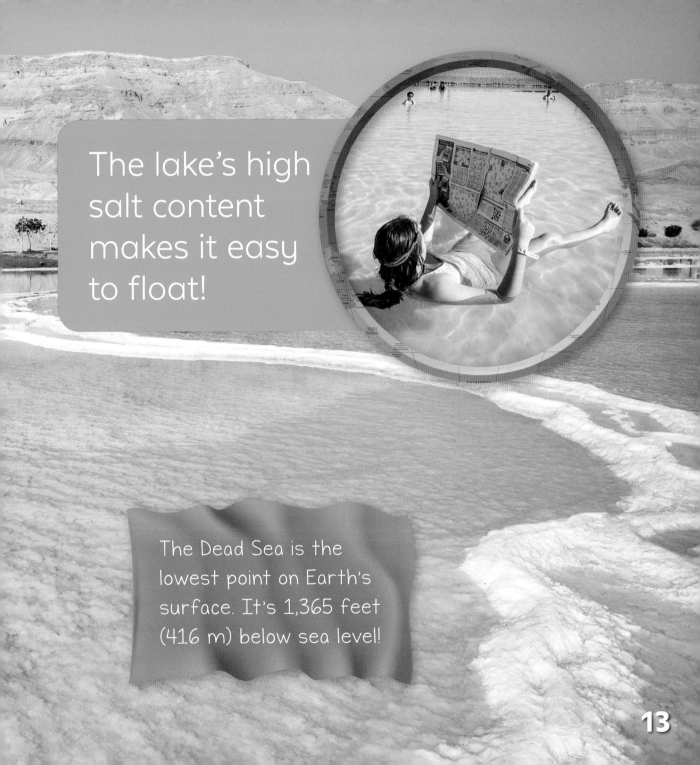

The lake's high salt content makes it easy to float!

The Dead Sea is the lowest point on Earth's surface. It's 1,365 feet (416 m) below sea level!

The history of Israel dates back thousands of years.

In 1948, the country was created as a homeland for Jewish people.

However, the Palestinian people were already living on the land.

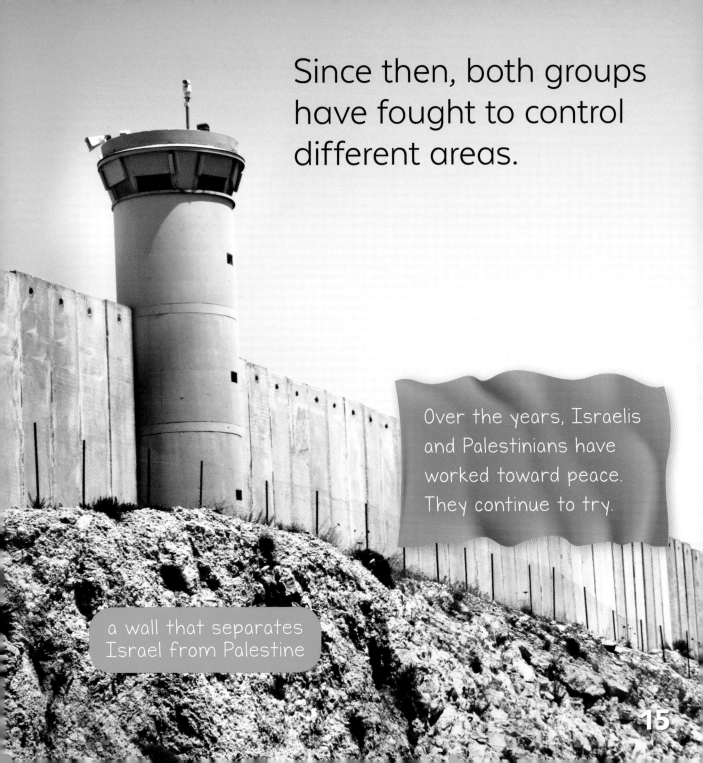

Since then, both groups have fought to control different areas.

Over the years, Israelis and Palestinians have worked toward peace. They continue to try.

a wall that separates Israel from Palestine

Jerusalem is the biggest city in Israel—and one of the oldest.

It dates back 5,000 years!

It's also the country's **capital**.

Jerusalem

Tel Aviv is the second biggest Israeli city.

Israel is a special place for **religious** people.

Jews, Muslims, and Christians all come here.

They visit the Temple Mount in Jerusalem.

It's one of the most holy spots.

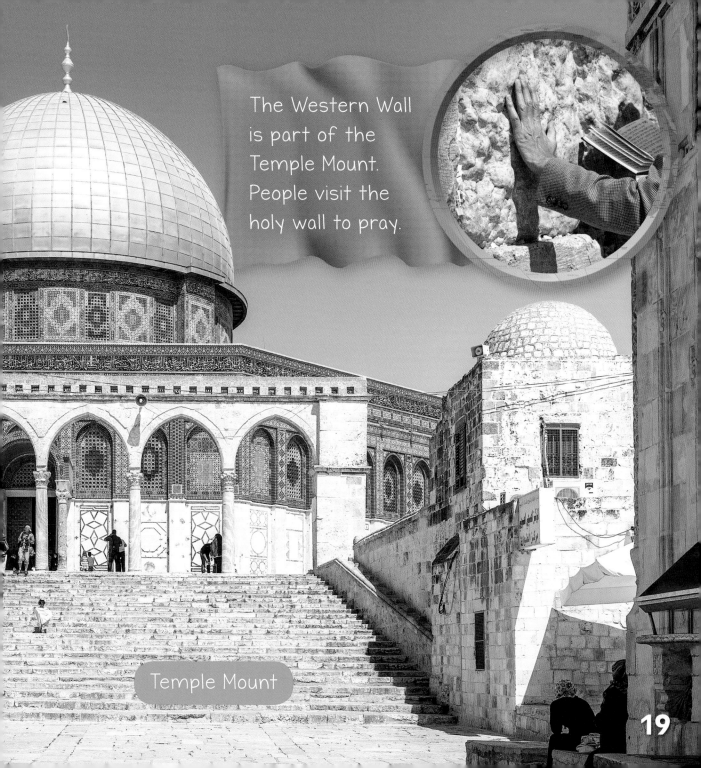

The Western Wall is part of the Temple Mount. People visit the holy wall to pray.

Temple Mount

19

Most of the people who live in Israel are Jewish.

Rosh Hashanah is the Jewish New Year.

shofar

To celebrate, Jews blow a ram's horn called a *shofar*.

Jews eat apples and honey on Rosh Hashanah.

dipping apple slices in honey

Everyone hopes it will be a sweet year!

Most people in Israel speak Hebrew.

This is how you say *hello* in Hebrew:

Hebrew writing

שלום
Shalom
(shah-LOHM)

This is how you say *thank you very much*:

תודה רבה
Toda Raba
(toh-DAH rah-BAH)

Many people living in Israel speak Arabic.

23

Israeli food is tasty.

Falafel is a fried ball made from chickpeas.

falafel sandwich

It's often tucked inside warm pita bread.

Bamba is a puffy snack. It's made from peanut butter.

Go team!

Israelis love soccer.

Fans cheer for their favorite players.

Israelis enjoy chess, too. Some of the world's best players are Israeli.

Israel is a popular place to visit. More than 3 million people travel there each year!

For its size, Israel has more **museums** than any other country.

Fast Facts

Capital city: Jerusalem

Population of Israel:
More than 8 million

Main languages:
Hebrew and Arabic

Money: Shekel

Major religions:
Judaism, Christianity, and Islam

Neighboring countries include:
Lebanon, Syria, Jordan, and Egypt

Cool Fact: Off the coast of Israel is a large **coral reef**. There, people can see colorful fish.

capital (KAP-uh-tuhl) a city where a country's government is based

coral reef (KOR-uhl REEF) a group of rocklike structures formed from the skeletons of sea animals called coral polyps

museums (myoo-ZEE-ums) places where objects of art, history, or science are displayed

national (NASH-uh-nuhl) having to do with a whole nation or country

religious (re-LIJ-uhs) very faithful

31

Index

Read More

Smith, Debbie. *Israel the People (Lands, Peoples, & Cultures).* New York: Crabtree (2007).

Washburn, Kim. *Jerusalem (Let's Go Explore).* New York: Zonderkidz (2014).

Learn More Online

To learn more about Israel, visit

www.bearportpublishing.com/CountriesWeComeFrom

About the Author

Thomas Persano likes to travel but has never been to Israel. One day, he would like to float in the Dead Sea.